Sort Your Shit Out

SORT YOUR SHIT OUT

An Hachette UK Company
www.hachette.co.uk

Vie Books, an imprint of Summersdale Publishers
Part of Octopus Publishing Group Limited
Carmelite House
50 Victoria Embankment
LONDON
EC4Y 0DZ
UK

www.summersdale.com

The authorized representative in the EEA is Hachette Ireland, 8 Castlecourt Centre, Castleknock Road, Castleknock, Dublin 15, D15 YF6A, Ireland

Printed and bound in China

ISBN: 978-1-83799-501-1

This FSC® label means that materials used for the product have been responsibly sourced

MIX
Paper | Supporting responsible forestry
FSC® C016973

Substantial discounts on bulk quantities of Summersdale books are available to corporations, professional associations and other organizations. For details contact general enquiries: telephone: +44 (0) 1243 771107 or email: enquiries@summersdale.com.

Sort Your Shit Out

How to Change Your Life by Tidying Up Your Stuff and Sorting Out Your Head Space

Vicki Vrint

CONTENTS

Introduction

Decluttering your life will change it for the better – you'll be able to see the living room floor again, for a start. But there's more to a decluttered lifestyle than being able to find the car keys without sending out a search party. Imagine relaxing in a calm and ordered home, surrounded by the things you really love. Imagine having the time – and space – to indulge in your hobbies without feeling that you should be doing something else instead. Wouldn't that be wonderful?

And once you sort out the physical clutter around you, it's much easier to organize other areas of your life too; the things you've been meaning to look at for ages, such as your career, friendships and finances.

Decluttering is a lot less complicated than you might think. All you need to do is:

1. Get rid of the stuff you don't need/love
2. Organize the stuff you do need/love
3. Have fun.

It really is that simple. So why do many of us find the idea intimidating? Our mistake is that we imagine tackling everything in one go, which can make it seem like an enormous task. Break the process down into manageable categories, however, and it's a piece of cake. Part One of this book shows you how to rationalize your belongings one category at a time. Soon your home will be clutter-free and you'll be itching to show off your newly organized surroundings.

Once you've decluttered your home, there'll be no stopping you from streamlining other aspects of your life too: updating your résumé, finding time to take that cookery course, sorting out your fitness regime and much more. It's just a case of following the same three steps: declutter, organize and enjoy. Part Two will focus more specifically on these areas, with plenty of tips to ensure that you make the most of your newly discovered free time.

So, what are you waiting for? Sort your shit out!

PART ONE

Sort Out Your Space

The first step to achieving a streamlined new life is to declutter the space around you. Tackle the different categories of clutter in your home one by one and you'll not only see immediate results, you'll also feel inspired to move on and tackle more. Before you know it, you'll be living in a calm and uncluttered environment and feeling revitalized. So read on and take the first step on your journey to clutter-free living.

REHOMING YOUR CLUTTER

As you declutter your home, you'll inevitably find yourself with bags and boxes of things that you no longer need. What should you do with it all?

- **Friends and family:** Does anyone you know need a foot spa?

- **eBay/Vinted:** For anything that can be easily posted.

- **Local online selling groups:** A great way to make some cash – and no delivery fees, because buyers will collect.

- **Freecycle, Freegle and other free recycling websites:** It's amazing how far people will travel for a free shoe rack, but beware of timewasters.

- **Car boot sales:** Do some research first as to what sells and which are the best sites.

- **Secondhand shops:** Books, clothes, alarming vases... Charity shops will be glad to take many things off your hands.

Clothes

It's easy to acquire more and more items of clothing as we get older, and surprisingly hard to ditch the things that we no longer wear. Whether it's for sentimental reasons or from a belief that we will slim down enough to wear that favourite shirt again one day, many of us suffer from bulging wardrobes and overstuffed drawers.

But never fear! Once you start to sort your shit out and de-junk your clothes chaos, you'll feel freer and lighter – and you'll actually be able to find your fashion favourites when you need them.

GETTING STARTED

Before you begin filling bin bags for your favourite secondhand shop, here are a few questions that will help you to sort the evergreens from the has-beens.

1. Do I love it?
2. Do I wear it?
3. Does it project the image I want to portray?
4. Does it itch or scratch?
5. Can I actually move in it comfortably?

Number 3 is the real "eureka" question for many people. Even if you love a particular piece of clothing, do you want other people to see you in it? If you're finding it hard to be an objective critic, enlist a friend who feels comfortable enough to tell you if something is wrong for you. Your storage space is limited, so it just doesn't make sense to waste your prime real estate on clothes you're not crazy about.

DECLUTTER THOSE DRAWERS

Once you've ejected all those items that you know you'll never wear again, it's time to revolutionize your storage habits. We tend to automatically stack our clothes in piles, but the downside of this is that we have to flip through them in order to find the perfect piece of clothing. Eventually, the pile gets messy and our long-lost best T-shirt sinks to the bottom, never to be seen again until the next big clear-out.

If you arrange your clothes by rolling them and standing them upright in the drawer, you'll be able to see all of your items at a glance, and a rainbow of T-shirts will be at your disposal every day.

TURN
THIS

INTO
THIS

FOR EVERY MINUTE SPENT IN ORGANIZING, AN HOUR IS EARNED.

BENJAMIN FRANKLIN

ORGANIZE YOUR OUTFITS

Bring a sense of order to your wardrobe by following these simple rules.

- Invest in some good hangers. Your clothes will look less crumpled, so no need to iron (hooray!).
- Hang items that go together on one hanger, so that you can grab an outfit quickly rather than choosing random garments and spending the day looking as if you got dressed in the dark.
- Organize your outfits in sections, by colour. Not only does this make it easier to find things, but you'll feel super smug every time you open your wardrobe.

When storing seasonal items, don't forget to weed out anything that you haven't worn recently. Also, remember to dry-clean certain items, such as winter coats, before putting them away.

SIMPLICITY BOILS DOWN TO TWO THINGS: IDENTIFY THE ESSENTIAL AND ELIMINATE THE REST.

LEO BABUTA

BED LINEN

Think back to the last time you put away your bed linen. Did you:

A. Neatly pop it into its designated place in the airing cupboard?

B. Wedge it in with a shoehorn? You just about closed the door but the next person to open it will get a pillowcase in the face.

C. Fail to fit it properly in the cupboard… or the overflow drawer…? Instead, you balanced it on top of the microwave, where it looks pretty darn attractive.

You are (presumably) running a home, not a hotel, so you don't need cupboards full of spare bed linen. Thin down your collection. Fold duvet covers around matching pillowcases so that you can grab a set in seconds and improve your bed linen storage experience. (And remember that if a horde of visitors does suddenly descend, you can always borrow bedding from friends.)

LIGHTENING THE LOAD

Washing and putting away your clothes is a bit of a chore, but if you let it get out of control, you'll soon find yourself surrounded by enough clothing for the entire von Trapp family. Save yourself time and effort by following these tips.

1. Pre-sort light and dark items using separate laundry baskets or baskets that have separate compartments.

2. Avoid as much ironing as possible by being careful when hanging items out to dry.

3. Hang similar items together – underwear, socks, etc. – then remove and fold easily into piles ready for putting away.

4. If you have children, make them responsible for putting away their own clothing. Try leaving the pile on their pillow or following them around with it until the job is done, unless you want your sofa disappearing beneath a mountainous heap of clothes.

HANDBAGS AND MANBAGS

You're heading out for the day, so you grab your bag and heave it onto your shoulder. Yes, it's a *bit* heavy... and you can't quite close the zip... and, now you mention it, the stitching on the strap looks a bit strained. But you're going to be out ALL DAY, and you might just need that hand sanitizer, eye mask or jar of pickles.

Many of us spend the day carrying around far more than we actually need: if your bag arm is twice the size of your other arm, you know you've got a problem.

Declutter your bag now: the receipts, the gunky mess that was once a boiled sweet and at least 30 of the 35 pens. Then make it a habit to go through your bag whenever you return to the house. It'll be a weight off your mind – and your shoulder too.

TOILETRIES AND BEAUTY EQUIPMENT

Take a look around your bathroom. There are probably clusters of bottles around the bathtub, unwanted Christmas gifts gathering dust on top of the cabinet and regiments of too-good-to-be-true lotions crammed into the cupboard. For many of us, this room is the only place where we can be alone, but rather than being a relaxing sanctuary, a cluttered bathroom can leave you feeling claustrophobic.

And the bathroom is not the only place where these items gather. Many of us have dressing tables stocked with scents and make-up, not to mention drawers full of items for improving our appearance. But do not worry! This area is one of the easiest to declutter.

GET MOTIVATED

Picture yourself on holiday. Picture your hotel room – it looks so clean and inviting, doesn't it? You've unpacked, but the dressing table is uncluttered, the floor is clear and the bathroom is a peaceful sanctum with just a few of your favourite products stored neatly in the cabinet.

One of the reasons we feel so relaxed on holiday – apart from the sun, sea and enormous prawns – is that we are not burdened by belongings. We have everything we need and yet we are not surrounded by piles of things to tidy. (Obviously, having cleaning services helps, too.)

Keep returning to this peaceful image as you sort your beauty shit out and bring a bit of five-star glamour to your bathroom.

GETTING STARTED

1. Empty each cupboard and group all similar products together; this way you can see just how many miracle volumizing shampoos you have collected.

2. Identify the products that you use regularly and – as long as you haven't stockpiled enough to get you through a nuclear fallout – keep them.

3. You will probably be left with items that fall into two categories.

   · Gifts: Someone thought about what you might like and got it spectacularly wrong, but you've said thank you anyway. These products have served their purpose. Ship them on out.

   · Products you've bought hoping that they'll make your hair grow, your skin glow or your teeth look whiter. You've tried them but they don't serve their purpose. Ship them on out, too. You're gorgeous as you are.

4. Designate a shelf for each type of product (or each person in the household) and put away your stash, placing frequently used products at the front.

MEDICINAL

BEAUTY

DENTAL

LET GO OR
BE DRAGGED.

ZEN PROVERB

PARTING WITH YOUR PRODUCTS

You've been ruthless and thinned out your toiletries, but what do you do with the items that you don't need? Well, if they're unopened, you can:

- Pass them on to friends who do like litres of lavender-scented body lotion
- Donate them to a secondhand shop
- Offer them to a care home or shelter.

If products have been opened but don't suit you, browse the internet to find other uses for them. Shampoo can be used for cleaning the toilet, for example, and toothpaste for whitening your trainers.

BEAUTY BITS AND BOBS

Scents, make-up, watches, jewellery: wherever these live in your home, they need to be organized. If you have a dressing table, it could well be covered in a mishmash of these objects, making it hard to track down what you need and a nightmare to keep clean. The best solution is to group things together.

Put all your perfumes or aftershave bottles on a small tray, or stand them in an attractive box so that you can move them easily for dusting.

In the case of jewellery and watches – unless they are valuable or need special care – it's best to store them in plain sight, as you'll be more likely to wear them. Use jewellery trees (or mug stands make a good alternative).

When it comes to make-up, hair accessories and belts, which are often stored in drawers, division is the key. Use small boxes (rather than pricey drawer dividers) to keep similar items together.

HAVE NOTHING IN YOUR HOUSE THAT YOU DO NOT KNOW TO BE USEFUL, OR BELIEVE TO BE BEAUTIFUL.

WILLIAM MORRIS

BOGUS BEAUTY EQUIPMENT

So, you saw an advert for this amazing device for curling/straightening/removing your hair/eyebrows/eyelashes (please don't try to remove your eyelashes) and you bought it... but now it's languishing in its box on top of your wardrobe or lurking in a drawer and gleaming at you menacingly whenever it catches your eye.

If you're the proud owner of a piece of beauty equipment that you never use, pass it on to someone who will and don't feel guilty about the wasted money. You've spent the cash and may not be able to recoup it (electrical items can be difficult to sell on, as you may be held liable if they turn out to be faulty), but don't waste your storage space on them, too.

> Electrical goods (marked with a crossed-out bin symbol) should never be thrown out with your general waste.

BETTER BEAUTY EQUIPMENT

For items that you do use regularly, strike a balance between having them ready to grab in a – usually hair-related – crisis and keeping them out of sight to give your home a streamlined look. (No matter how much you love your new curling wand, you don't want it to be the centrepiece on the buffet table when you have friends over.) Find these items an easy-to-access drawer and store them (in their boxes, if it's necessary to keep add-ons together). You can always cut out the top of the box so that you can get them in and out more easily.

OLD MEDICINES

So, years ago, someone in your household – let's just call them X – suffered from piles/cold sores/thrush/nits (hopefully not all at once). Now, months later, a cracked tube of X's miracle remedy is still languishing in the bathroom cabinet, along with several half-completed courses of antibiotics and cough syrup that belong in a museum.

Do we really need to congest our cupboards with these reminders of past ailments just in case things flare up again? Well, no, we don't. And if the worst does happen, let's push the boat out and treat ourselves to a brand new tube of cream.

Never get rid of old medicines down the toilet or sink. Take them to your local pharmacy, where they will be disposed of safely.

Paperwork

Although a lot of our personal admin can be taken care of online, a surprising amount of paperwork still piles up around the house: receipts, statements, the handbook for that angle grinder. If you don't have a system for sorting these documents, they can soon take over any flat surface they find. (On the plus side, though, covering things with paper does cut down on the dusting.)

Sorting your administrative shit out is easy, though, and enormously satisfying – especially if you own a cross-cut shredder. (Just don't shred the instruction manual first.)

THE SECRET OF GETTING AHEAD IS GETTING STARTED.

MARK TWAIN

GETTING STARTED

Going through mountains of documents can seem like an onerous task but tackle it in these three steps and you'll soon be in paperwork heaven.

1. **Declutter:** Work out which papers you really need to keep copies of (see page 35).

2. **Develop a filing system:** Yes, like visiting the dentist, filing papers is intensely boring, a bit scary and sometimes painful – but it's also necessary.

3. **Get into good paperwork habits:** With a little discipline, even the most hardened admin-phobe can get into a good routine and stop piles of paperwork blocking access to important things, such as the front door.

PRUNING YOUR PAPERS

Sit down with a hot drink and your paperwork mountain. Weed out the rubbish: brochures, takeaway menus and leaflets for places you'll never visit. Enjoy the pleasing thump they make as they hit the bottom of the recycling bin.

Set aside all the important stuff ready to file: official certificates, passports, wills, insurance documents, financial paperwork, medical information, payslips and other tax-related things.

Whatever's left over may well have sentimental value, but try not to hold on to every birthday card you've ever received or every letter from your aunt. Cherry-pick your favourites and keep them in a mementos box out of the way. (Stay on top of this stash in future. If you can fit something in the box then you can keep it; if not, you'll need to sacrifice it – or something else – to make room.)

TO KEEP OR NOT TO KEEP

Many of us hold on to more paperwork than we need. Think twice before putting the following items away in your new, super-slim filing cabinet.

- **Bank statements:** Go paperless if possible. You can still check your statements regularly online and berate yourself for buying that expensive pair of shoes.

- **Receipts:** File receipts for high-value purchases (furniture, jewellery, appliances, etc.) in one folder. Keep receipts for day-to-day purchases in a bulldog clip and ditch them every month or so.

- **Warranties and user guides:** Go through your collection and get rid of any that you no longer need. (It's not that hard to use a kettle.) Bear in mind that you can access information on how to use most gadgets online. File anything that you must keep in another folder.

A STREAMLINED SYSTEM

If you haven't already got one, set up a filing cabinet, drawer or concertina file and clearly mark the dividers. (Avoid stacking too much paperwork in boxes or you'll end up spending hours burrowing around for that elusive swimming certificate.)

File all your official bits and pieces, but remember that you don't need to hold on to everything forever.

- Bills: Deal with them, file them and keep them for two years max.
- Insurance documents: Keep them for as long as they are valid and then discard.
- Work/tax documents: Keep payslips and tax-related documents for two years from the end of the tax year they relate to. For self-employment and small business records, hold on to documents for six years after you file each tax return.

WHAT THE WORLD REALLY NEEDS IS MORE LOVE AND LESS PAPERWORK.

PEARL BAILEY

STAYING ON TOP

Stay on top of your paperwork with these handy tips:

- Action things immediately or add a note to your diary/phone to sort them within the next few days.
- Shred documents straightaway. Do not let a shredding pile accumulate or you will be back to square one!
- Keep a single folder or in tray for items that are awaiting your attention, but be scrupulous about NOT using it as a dumping ground for random bits of paper.

Use your shredded paper for packing parcels, kindling the fire or adding to the compost heap. If you're feeling crafty, you can even make handmade paper with it. Shredded paper makes good cat litter too, but will need changing more frequently than shop-bought products.

LEAFLETS

Loft insulation brochures, leaflets on skydiving, takeaway food menus... If they're not invading our homes via the letterbox, we're picking up this literary litter ourselves and bringing it back to fill our recycling bins.

Opt out of receiving the unaddressed leaflets delivered to you by putting a "No Junk Mail" sign on your front door or mailbox and don't pick up random brochures on your travels. (If the day comes when you really want to find someone new to launder your llama's blankets, you can always check the internet.)

And, no, you'll never get round to installing a Jacuzzi in the conservatory, so throw out that leaflet too!

CYBERCLUTTER

We often handle our bills and banking online, so it's important to organize our cyberclutter too. If you have an idle 5 minutes at your computer, try one of these quick fixes... and then let yourself succumb to that YouTube video of cats leaping out of cupboards.

- Tidy up your desktop. Delete or file any images or documents that you've left scattered around and which are now obscuring your carefully chosen desktop picture.
- Go through your inbox and delete or file old emails.
- Back up your photos or important documents.
- Unsubscribe from emails that you no longer read (or didn't request in the first place).
- Clear your cache or delete old call logs from your phone.
- Tidy up your browser bookmarks.

STUDY NOTES

Courses come with plenty of paperwork, but if you get yourself organized, you're much more likely to achieve the results you deserve. It's important to have an area set aside just for study, however compact. Make sure that it's quiet and well lit, with space for you to work and keep materials to hand. (You don't want to have to move the ironing board and hedge trimmer every time you sit down to study.)

Start by clearing your desk completely and then get together all of your notes. Organize them into binders, using one per topic with dividers for subsections. (An index of topics at the front will help, too.) Store these and then set up your other essentials: writing equipment, laptop, a clock, a noticeboard for timetables, etc. Ditch or rehome anything else and keep your study area clean. Job done!

BOOKS

For many of us, books are like old friends: faithful companions that provide a safe haven in times of trouble. But if you accept friendship requests from every battered paperback you find on your travels, you'll end up with bookcases bulging with dusty tomes and a reading pile that makes you feel intimidated rather than invigorated.

So grab a duster and sort your literary shit out, one shelf at a time. You'll soon transform your chaotic collection into an ordered and appealing library, and you'll feel less guilty about relaxing with a book next time you have half an hour to spare.

GETTING STARTED

Don't try to declutter your bookshelves by randomly searching for individual books to throw away. You'll spend half an hour fondly running your finger along their spines before finding just one item for your sacrificial pile – probably belonging to someone else – and needing a little lie down to recover.

You're going to have to be brave and take all the books off your shelves at once! If you have a huge collection, it's a good idea to gather together all books in one category at a time, so you can make an informed decision. I mean how many regency romances do you really need?

Now go through and decide which books you absolutely must keep: beautiful books, books that move you and books that contain a loving inscription from someone special. If they deserve a place in your heart, they deserve a place on your bookshelf.

LITERARY LIES

You've identified your keepers and now it's time to sort out the rest of your fiction collection. The books you'll definitely read (or re-read) deserve a permanent home, but be honest about which these might be. Many of us have shelves of novels that we're planning to read someday, but for most of these babies "someday" will never come. Restrict yourself to keeping a dozen or so books that you're dying to curl up with, and you'll feel a buzz of excitement at being able to choose your next read at a glance.

Charity shops are grateful recipients of books, especially paperbacks. You can also find book bins by many bottle banks – a handy option for dropping off your literary leftovers outside business hours.

INFORMATION OVERLOAD

For some of us it's cookery books; for others it's science, travel or the history of dentistry. Whatever your non-fiction crush, your well-stocked library will contain dozens of volumes about it, and a few other subjects too, all bought in a quest to expand your mind. But reference books aren't small and chances are you've ended up expanding your bookshelves, too.

Be ruthless and sort through your collection, keeping only the books that you refer to regularly, such as titles relevant to your work or studies.

Before you load up your car with all those reference books, have a think about why you've been stockpiling them. If you own 20 books on graphic design and hate working as an electrician, your tomes may be trying to tell you something!

SHELVING SECRETS

Books bring life and character to a room. Once you've decluttered and regrouped them, you can enjoy displaying them (and removing them from the shelves without creating an avalanche and knocking yourself out). Grouping together all the titles by spine colour can look very effective; alternatively, a series of related titles displayed on a single shelf somewhere quirky will look good too.

If – despite your best decluttering efforts – you still find yourself with a few extra books to shelve, remember that many bookcases are fairly deep and you can double up with a second row of hidden gems behind the first. You could even stack a column of books in a corner, as this takes up minimal floor space.

ESSENTIAL
READING

AFTER ORGANIZING
YOUR BOOKCASE, YOU
MAY FIND YOU HAVE NEW
STORAGE OPTIONS

THE BOOK MUST OF
NECESSITY BE PUT
INTO A BOOKCASE.
AND THE BOOKCASE
MUST BE HOUSED.
AND THE HOUSE
MUST BE KEPT. AND
THE LIBRARY MUST
BE DUSTED, MUST
BE ARRANGED, MUST
BE CATALOGUED.

WILLIAM EWART GLADSTONE

CLUTTER OFFENDER #4
MAGAZINES

It's great when you discover that there's a magazine devoted to your hobby, however obscure it might be. Trouble is, soon your favourite knitting/railway/concrete mag is not just out there on the newsagents' shelves – it's in your home, too, piled knee-deep on the stairs.

Magazines are a luxury. They give us an excuse to take time out and indulge our interests, so parting with them can be a bit of a wrench. But, if we're honest, few of us ever revisit old issues of magazines. It's best to cut out any essential articles (if you must!) and then pass the magazines on to another concrete enthusiast. (If you don't know anyone else who shares your hobby, doctors and dental surgeries, nursing homes and libraries may be interested in rehoming your reading material.)

Craft and Hobby Supplies

Unless your hobby involves building furniture for ants, it's likely to need a lot of bulky equipment of some sort. Finding a home for your sewing machine can be tricky enough, but if you're into glassblowing or horse riding, storing your kit (not to mention your horse) can be even more of a challenge.

Most of us have limited time to spare for our hobbies and we don't want to waste a precious half-hour unpacking the garage to search for an essential piece of equipment. It's time to get creative and think outside the (craft) box: with a little planning, a small space can be transformed into a hobbies heaven.

START WHERE
YOU ARE. USE
WHAT YOU
HAVE. DO WHAT
YOU CAN.

ARTHUR ASHE

GET MOTIVATED

Think back to the moment when you first fell in love with your favourite hobby. Perhaps you overheard a piece of music years ago and decided to learn to play the cello? Or maybe a photo of a mystery relative sent you rushing off to explore the branches of your family tree? What was it that excited you about your new hobby? How did you picture yourself carrying it out? Visualize this.

Chances are you're seeing yourself in an uncluttered haven (possibly bathed in golden light, depending on how cinematic you're feeling). You are relaxed and happy and have all you need to hand as you put the finishing touches to your lovingly taxidermized rat. Take a moment to enjoy these feelings before returning to reality. Now, repeat after me: "There is no reason why I can't recreate this vision in real life."

GETTING STARTED

First Rule of Hobby Club: If you don't have your equipment to hand, you'll never use it.

Second Rule of Hobby Club: If you keep your equipment to hand, your house will look like it's been reverse-burgled by a crazed haberdasher.

Think about your priorities.

- Do you need all of those different pastels/circuit boards/model tanks? If you slim down your collection, you may be able to find it a permanent home.

- If you have multiple hobbies, can you focus on different ones at different times of the year and store out-of-season equipment out of the way?

- Is there anything you can get rid of to make way for some valuable hobby space? (Preferably an item of furniture rather than a member of your household!)

CHANGING SPACES

Most of us can't afford to convert the attic, garage or shed into an exclusive hobbies den – although if you can, please go ahead... and have you got room to store some guitars? – but it might be possible to adapt a smaller area of your home for your indoor hobby. Check online sites, such as Pinterest, for inspiration and think about the following.

- **Under the stairs:** Removing an understairs cupboard can leave space for a desk and bespoke storage shelves.
- **Built-in cupboards:** With the doors removed, these can house a work surface, storage and shelving.
- **Corridors or landings:** You may be able to fit a small, strategically placed table into one of these spaces, with storage above or below it.

CRAFTY THINKING

Craft collections can easily expand beyond their designated drawers or boxes. Keep them under control by following these tips.

- Be realistic about which materials you will use and avoid stockpiling them.

- If you have more than four items of something, they need a container. Buy multiple boxes, jars or pots and organize your stash. Label everything!

- Look out for packaging that you could reuse. Multipacks of socks and underpants sometimes come in handy bags that are great for storing smaller items such as yarns.

- Search secondhand shops for quirky cabinets, racks or storage chests that can house crafty bits and bobs.

- Visit craft outlets or browse the internet for creative storage ideas.

TAKING TIME OUT

Outdoor hobbies often involve larger items of equipment that can be difficult to store. You don't want to have to receive parcels (or visitors) through the living room window because you've got a stripped-down motorcycle engine clogging up your hallway. Think about the following suggestions.

- Buddying up: Find a pal who is into the same hobby. Perhaps they have storage space you could share?
- Hiring or borrowing larger items (particularly if you don't use them often).
- Storing items elsewhere: Set up a shed or summer house for your hobby supplies or look into renting a storage unit.

If you're thinking of taking up a new outdoor hobby, why not try an introductory course first, over a few weeks if possible, to find out whether it really appeals and it's worth you investing in expensive gear.

FOOD AND COOKING EQUIPMENT

In most homes, the kitchen is storage central. With wall-to-wall cupboards, drawers and a growing trend for enormous fridge-freezers, there should be plenty of space to keep everything we need. So why do many of us end up with cluttered worktops or items piled on top of our cabinets?

We're exposed to so many multi-buy bargains on food, not to mention time-saving kitchen gadgets, that it's easy to give in to our inner hoarder and overstock our cupboards and drawers. But don't lose heart: decluttering the kitchen is fun.

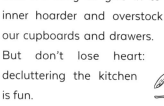

CLUTTER IS POSTPONED DECISIONS.

BARBARA HEMPHILL

GETTING STARTED

As with any area of the house, decluttering is essential to achieving a calm and ordered space, but before you seize that dusty yoghurt maker, take some time to think about your kitchen layout. What works – and, more importantly, what doesn't work – at the moment? A few minutes spent assessing this now could lead to a time-saving brainwave.

- Are there any areas where clutter currently builds up? What type of clutter is it? Who is putting it there? (How will you punish the offender?!) And where can you store this stuff instead?

- Is workspace an issue? Do you have any rarely used appliances taking up valuable room? Do you have space for an island or trolley that could expand your work area?

- Do you find yourself forever trailing from one side of the kitchen to the other? Would storing things in different cupboards make a difference?

HOW CAN
YOU GOVERN
A COUNTRY
WHICH HAS
246 VARIETIES
OF CHEESE?

CHARLES DE GAULLE

STREAMLINING YOUR SUPPLIES

Perhaps stockpiling food is a primal instinct, but these days we really don't need to stuff our freezers with enough pizza to keep us going until the next successful mammoth hunt. Here are some tips on how to slim down your food hoard.

1. Go through your store cupboards. Discard anything that's out of date.

2. Restack your cupboards by placing items that are closer to their use-by date at the front (alphabetizing your tins is optional).

3. Do a stocktake of your fridge and freezer. Discard anything that you don't remember buying, can't identify or will never eat.

4. Put back your remaining fridge and freezer supplies. (Use a large plastic container to keep smaller items together.)

5. Plan your week's meals in advance and shop online to guard against impulse purchases.

SHORT-DATE
ITEMS AT THE FRONT

LOOSE ITEMS COLLECTED
IN A CONTAINER

GADGETS

It's tempting, isn't it? It's a waffle maker, and means that every morning you can have fresh waffles! (They'll be great with the fresh orange juice from that juicer you never use.) And if you buy it now, you'll get the banana slicer free!

If you're not careful, appliances can take over your kitchen and, before you know it, you'll find yourself with an army of chrome occupying your worktop and barely enough space left over to butter a postage stamp.

Assess your appliances. Make space on your worktop for the items that you use weekly; put anything you use less often in an easy-to-access spot out of sight, and get rid of your ill-chosen and irrational purchases. If you really fancy a posh breakfast, visit a restaurant and let them store (and clean) the waffle iron.

MAXIMIZING YOUR STORAGE

If you've got money to splurge, adapting your kitchen to include the latest storage solutions will maximize your space. Pull-out corner cupboard racks are an old favourite, but did you know that you can have drawers fitted behind the kick plates under your kitchen units, for example? You don't need to spend big, though. Look for any areas of wasted space and see if you can squeeze some sneaky storage into them.

- Can you fit a magazine rack inside a cupboard and use it for storing chopping boards or baking sheets vertically?
- Would a hanging rack or rail free up some cupboard space if you used it for pots and pans?
- Could you hang whisks, etc. on the inside of a cupboard door?

Remember to store things near to where you use them.

CLUTTER OFFENDER #5
NOVELTY MUGS

It might be chipped and stained, but you've still got that Star Wars mug you were given for your tenth birthday... and that "hilarious" one from your coworker that lost its comedy value before you threw the wrapping paper out. Why, oh why, do we hold on to this sort of thing? Take a look at your mug collection and then apply the following calculation:

Number of mugs ÷ Number of people in your household = ?

Is your answer more than three? WHY?! (And, no, you're NEVER going to have that many visitors all at once.)

If you find it too painful to choose between "The Boss" and "Keep Calm and Drink Coffee", get a friend to help. Using a third party to do the deed can be the easiest approach.

KEEPING IT CLEAR

In the kitchen, more than anywhere else, you need "A System".

- If you live with others, divide up the chores and make sure that everyone knows what they have to do – and make sure they do it.

- Draw up a list of Kitchen Rules. Pin it somewhere prominent, make it your screensaver, tattoo it on everyone's hands or sneak it into your partner's lunch box (thoughtful touches like this keep a relationship alive).

- Police your streamlined kitchen and adopt a zero-tolerance policy to clutter offenders. (That includes you!)

- Put things away as soon as you have finished with them.

- No, really... PUT THINGS AWAY AS SOON AS YOU HAVE FINISHED WITH THEM.

Tools and DIY Equipment

Even those of us who are not into DIY need a certain amount of equipment to keep our homes ticking over – ladders, buckets, an assortment of incorrectly sized screwdrivers, etc. – but whether it's stashed under the stairs or shoved in the shed, it's important to organize your DIY hoard.

If you're lucky enough to have a garden, you may well have a shed, but chances are it's packed floor-to-ceiling with garden paraphernalia. Spaces like this are all too easy to fill with clutter, but decluttering them is easy, too.

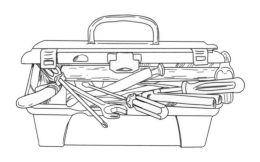

GETTING STARTED

Start by identifying your essential tools and equipment, and thinking about where they are kept. Maybe you find yourself balancing precariously on a bar stool because the ladder is buried in the shed? Or perhaps you have a cupboard full of items waiting to be mended because the superglue is hidden under the stairs. Rethink where these items live, then find an accessible cupboard for a few emergency essentials:

- A well-equipped toolbox, plugs and fuses, fire extinguisher
- Torch, batteries, candles and matches, first-aid kit
- Contact numbers for the plumber, electrician, etc.

Once you have these in place, you'll not only feel super-organized but probably a bit disappointed that you don't have an emergency to handle straightaway.

DECLUTTERING YOUR SHED

If you plan ahead, sorting your shed can be a therapeutic and satisfying task.

1. Think about the purpose of your shed. Is it simply for storing tools and equipment? Do you want to use it as a workshop? Are you hoping to take a break from your partner in it? Plan your storage/lighting/fittings accordingly.

2. Get together any storage solutions you need: shelving, pegboards, wall-mounted racks for long-handled tools, etc.

3. Pick a sunny day and remove everything from your shed in one go. (Yes, even the spiders!)

4. Discard broken items and anything you know you'll never use. (Be ruthless. You can always hire or borrow tools that you only need once in a while.)

5. Sweep your shed (wear a mask if it's very dusty) and then install any racks or shelving.

6. Put everything away, placing larger, less frequently used items at the back.

WHAT TO WEED OUT

When sorting out your hoard, get rid of the following:

- Broken tools
- Tools that you don't use
- Cracked plant pots
- Leftover materials that have gathered dust
- Almost-empty tins of paint (these take up valuable space and will only dry out, so make a note of the colours and buy tester pots for retouching)
- Old paint brushes
- Weird objects that you can't identify.

TIDY TOOLS

Although diehard DIYers can build up an impressive stash of tools, large and small, once you've decluttered your collection, storing it will be easy. Not only will you have the skill to pop up an extra shelf or two, but you'll also have the creativity to adapt and reuse items to provide some storage solutions of your own.

- Go to town with shelves or pegboards mounted on walls and store as many small tools as possible out of the way.
- Reuse household items: for example, a cutlery tray to organize a tool drawer and tin cans or margarine tubs for storing smaller items.
- Attach jar lids to the base of a shelf and use the (suspended) jars to store screws, nails, etc.
- Cut down leftover lengths of pipe, fix to a handy surface and use to store paintbrushes.
- Hang tool belts on the wall, and store bits and pieces in the pockets.

PEGBOARD STORAGE CAN
REVOLUTIONIZE YOUR COLLECTION

USE LEFTOVER HOUSEHOLD TUBS
AND BOXES FOR SMALL ITEMS

WE SHALL NOT
FAIL OR FALTER;
WE SHALL NOT
WEAKEN OR
TIRE... GIVE
US THE TOOLS,
AND WE WILL
FINISH THE JOB.

WINSTON CHURCHILL

CLUTTER OFFENDER #6
CHARGERS, PLUGS AND CORDS

You know the drawer I mean… The one you can't open because it's filled with a jumble of freaky black electrical spaghetti: old phone chargers, SCART leads and the surplus cables that come with every device you purchase. Hopefully, the reason you've held on to this clutter is that you know you can't throw it out with your everyday waste. But what can you do with it?

There aren't many options for reusing this type of stuff unless you fancy making quirky macramé belts. Plugs are painful to tread on, though, so you could try scattering them prongs-up in the corridor to catch burglars unawares. Alternatively, try local charities or electrical retailers, who may offer a recycling service, or take unwanted electrical things to the tip.

FAMILY CLUTTER

Every member of your household (adult, child or pet) brings a raft of possessions – and potential clutter – into the homestead until, before you know it, you're wading through a sea of sports kit, toys and kitty litter. Sorting your shit out as a family can seem like a challenge too far, but since the only other option – selling your family members on eBay – is illegal, you're going to need to take action.

How will you get everyone to agree to the clutter cull? Well, take some time to explain the benefits of decluttering to everyone and you'll soon have the team on board. So grasp the nettle – and some bin bags – and crack down on family clutter with the help of these simple tips.

THINGS
DON'T MATTER,
PEOPLE DO.

ROSIE THOMAS

GETTING STARTED

Before you start sifting through the family's cupboards, it's worth taking a little time to get everyone's support.

- Explain that a decluttered home will mean:
    - more space for storing/using favourite items
    - less time spent cleaning/searching for things
    - far fewer stressful mornings trying to get out of the door on time.

- Lead by example. Declutter "your" area and other family members may well covet your tidy space – just don't let them clutter it up again.

- Make decluttering a game. Younger children often find moving things around tremendously exciting. Form a human chain to empty the understairs cupboard or challenge the little ones to see how many loose coins they can collect from around the house.

- Make a plan of action. Get everyone to write down an area that they think should be tackled and start with these.

TOO MANY TOYS

Toys are obviously the main source of children's clutter. With Christmas presents, birthdays (including presents from everyone in your child's class, if they've had a party) and hand-me-downs from friends, it's very easy to let toys take over the whole house, however hard you try to corral them into one area.

Set a reasonable amount of storage aside for each child and help them to downsize their belongings to fit that. Some children may like the idea of donating outgrown items to charity, while others may be motivated by the thought of having space for whatever new acquisition has captured their imagination. While it is lovely to involve older children in the decision-making, there is no harm in tidying away your tot's abandoned or forgotten toys for a while and then rehoming these if they are not missed.

PERILOUS PLAYTHINGS

Child's age	Toy type	If you stand on it, it...
0-3 years	Large colourful lumps of plastic	Squeaks
4-8 years	Smaller colourful lumps of plastic	Hurts
9+ years	"Toys" now come with a charger and a health warning	Costs a month's salary to replace

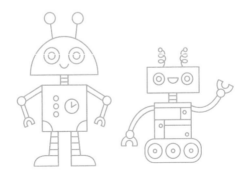

HIDE AND STORE

If you like to keep a few of your child's toys in the living room, get kids into the habit of tidying things away at the end of the day, so that you can enjoy the evening in an uncluttered environment. A smart toy chest or set of sturdy stackable boxes can hold a surprising amount of playthings. Or why not slide an under-bed drawer under the sofa as extra toy storage, if you have room?

You may be reluctant to break up large building block playsets and other similar toys, which can take your little one (and you) many hours of hard work to construct, so find a suitable-sized storage box for these and store them in all their assembled glory.

THE CHILD'S TOYS AND THE OLD MAN'S REASONS ARE THE FRUITS OF THE TWO SEASONS.

WILLIAM BLAKE

KIDS' DRAWINGS AND CRAFTS

It may feel a bit unkind to call your little ones' masterpieces clutter – what with every artwork being an expression of their unique personality, and all – but once you've seen a dozen sketches of princesses or dinosaurs, it's only natural for your enthusiasm to wane. It's just as well that most of us adults don't carry on knocking out paintings, stories and cardboard models at the same rate as children – we'd be up to our ears in paper and glue!

Pick a few items to display and then quietly recycle the other random sketches that make their way home. You could hang some washing line or string up and help the kids to peg up their favourite pieces. For the sake of your own sanity, refresh your gallery regularly.

GRAB AND GO

You're ready to leave the house in time for that appointment except... Where are the car keys?! You had them yesterday... You know because THAT'S HOW YOU DROVE THE CAR HOME! There's nothing worse than being held up by a frantic last-minute search for something essential. Avoid these stressful moments by making sure that these items are always kept somewhere convenient for you to grab and go.

- Put door keys, car keys, etc. in a bowl or hang them on a rack in the hall (out of sight of the front door).
- If you have a hallway, a free-standing shoe rack might be a good choice - you can store other seasonal items on top in wicker baskets/containers.
- Keep winter hats, scarves and gloves ready to grab in winter, and replace with sun cream, sunglasses and sun hats in the summer, packing away the out-of-season gear.

SCHOOL STUFF AND SPORTS GEAR

It's great that children get the opportunity to try out so many sports and activities, but with swimming on Mondays, fencing on Tuesdays, clarinet on Wednesdays and – hang on, what's on Thursday again? – they tend to accumulate so much stuff that they could do with their own porter and baggage trolley.

If you have room to hang pegs for them at a suitable height in the hallway then do so, and make sure that book bags, sports kits and coats live here – and here alone. (And enjoy the added challenge of not impaling yourself on the hooks.) If lunch boxes and water bottles have an assigned place too, you'll avoid dashing around looking for them at zero hour.

For other sports paraphernalia, try to keep a designated bag for each child's swim kit, football gear, etc., with the basics stored in it and – if possible – stash these in one place so that everything is easy to find.

PHOTOS, GIFTS AND KEEPSAKES

Some of our belongings tug at the heartstrings: photos from childhood, souvenirs from our first trip abroad... But if we hold on to every dog-eared print or novelty key ring, our keepsake collection can take over the home.

Go through boxes of photos and discard any that are blurred, duplicates or pictures you can't identify. Sort the rest chronologically and store them in albums or boxes. (Organize your digital pics by doing the same thing: delete any duff images and store the keepers in folders marked with the month or year. Don't forget to back them up, too.)

For gifts and keepsakes, think carefully about whether items a) serve a purpose or b) enhance your life. If they do neither but you're holding on to them because you would feel guilty giving them away, be strong! You deserve a home filled with things you love and these objects deserve a home where someone else will love them. Pass them on!

PART TWO

Sort Out Your Life

You've done it! You've sent carloads of books to the secondhand shop and you've been through your teapot collection with a fine-toothed comb. Your home is clutter-free and you're already feeling lighter, brighter and super-excited about the next step in your journey: sorting out your life.

As with decluttering your home, streamlining the other areas of your life is best achieved in a series of simple steps. If you turn your new-found decluttering skills to one area at a time, you'll find that – whether you're considering your studies, friendships or fitness – working out your priorities and achieving your goals will be a breeze.

Goals

Living a life without goals is like taking a journey without a map, satnav or even a destination in mind: you'll end up in a different place from where you started, but you'll never really know if it's the best place for you... and you'll have missed out on a lot of fun stuff along the way.

Goals give us something to aim for and focus on. Whether you've always wanted to learn to scuba dive or you dream of retraining and starting a new career, now is the time to nurture your aspirations and give them the attention they deserve. By focusing fully on things that motivate us, we can tap into our passion and find the resources we need to achieve our ambitions. Setting some goals is a brilliant way to do this.

A GOAL IS
A DREAM WITH
A DEADLINE.

NAPOLEON HILL

SETTING YOUR GOALS

You may already have some life goals in mind, but a vague desire is not going to get the job done. By writing your targets down, you'll be able to focus on the specifics of what you want and how to achieve it.

1. Write down headings for the different areas of your life. These might include career, home, hobbies, travel, family, health, friendships, love, finances, study, personal development, fun, etc.

2. Think about each area in turn and make a note of what you'd like to change or achieve. (Don't worry if you draw a blank for some areas; just concentrate on those that inspire you.)

3. Be as specific as you can and try to finish the exercise with a clearly written goal for each of your chosen topics.

4. Now write these goals out together as one list and pin it somewhere prominent to keep you motivated.

A QUESTION OF PRIORITIES

You have your list of goals and you're raring to go, but what should you tackle first? If one item on your list really leapt out (it's probably the one you underlined, wrote in capitals and surrounded with asterisks), that's obviously the place to start; if your winner wasn't so clearly defined, though, a good way to choose is to, literally, go with your gut.

Consider each of your goals in turn but pay attention to how you feel as you do so. Our emotional reactions can often be felt as a physical sensation in the body: does your stomach clench when you think about sorting out that thorny relationship with your colleague at work? Or do you feel your heart racing when you think about your plans to finally go travelling? If your head can't help you decide which path to follow first, your heart (or stomach) might be able to show you the way.

BREAKING IT DOWN

Right! You're going to do it! You're going to set up that pottery business in your back garden, but before you tell your boss exactly what you think of them and bulldoze the shed to make space for your studio, take some time to think about the nitty-gritty. The best way to achieve your goals is to break them down into smaller steps.

Write down, one step at a time, what you'll need to do to reach your aim. For example: do some internet research, talk to the council about planning permission, visit someone who has carried out a similar project, get recommendations for builders, source equipment, sort out the electrics, and so on. Now go back to the very first item on your to-do list and do it today.

GOING FOR GOALS

Don't let procrastination hold you back. It's time for some tough love.

Reason for procrastinating	It's a bad reason because...
"I might fail."	The only way you can be sure of failing is by never even trying. Do it anyway!
"I don't have time to do it."	You can and must make time if something is important to you. Do it anyway!
"If I wait long enough, someone else might sort it out for me."	They won't. Do it anyway (yourself)!
"I need to wait until I've got time to do it properly."	You'll still be saying that in 10 years' time. Take it step by step and do it anyway!
"I'm afraid I might succeed! What will happen if this actually works out?"	A new and exciting stage of your life will begin and you'll have new plans to look forward to. Do it anyway!

TO REACH A PORT, WE MUST SAIL – SAIL, NOT TIE AT ANCHOR – SAIL, NOT DRIFT.

FRANKLIN D. ROOSEVELT

STAYING MOTIVATED

It can be easier to encourage others in their plans than to motivate ourselves, so getting a support team in place can be a good way of working towards your goals. Maybe you have friends who have plans of their own? You needn't be going for the same goal: one person may be keen to start a new health regime, while someone else may want to change their job or study for a new qualification. What matters is that you find a time to meet regularly and update one another on your progress. Even if it's a quick 15-minute chat after work or a coffee on a Saturday morning, you'll come away feeling boosted by their enthusiasm and advice, and they'll feel the same way, too.

Set up a chat or email group and keep everyone posted about that meeting with the bank/boss/mother-in-law... but stay focused! Don't let your social-networking time turn into an evening of sharing cute panda videos. Knowing that your friends are rooting for you will be a great boost and will keep you on track.

MANAGING YOUR TIME

Time is our most precious commodity (well, apart from oxygen). We live such busy lives that it often seems there aren't enough hours in the day to get everything done. When we're juggling work, chores and family responsibilities – and trying to find time for our friends, hobbies and exercise, too – we can end up feeling exhausted by the end of the week and deflated because we haven't ticked everything off our to-do list.

Well, don't worry: if you've decluttered your home, you'll find that you've already saved yourself time every day (no more searching for missing items, and less time spent tidying up and cleaning), but you can do even better than that! By decluttering your schedule and trying out these time-saving tips, you can carve out even more time to spend doing the things that you really enjoy.

TIME IS A CREATED THING. TO SAY "I DON'T HAVE TIME" IS LIKE SAYING "I DON'T WANT TO."

LAO TZU

WHERE DOES ALL THE TIME GO?

When you're rushing headlong from one task to the next, it can be difficult to get a picture of how you're spending your time, so make a time chart to record what you've done each day for a week. Use a diary to note down what you do throughout the day and how long you spend doing it. Be as specific as possible: you were at work for 8 hours but did you make a note of your breaks and the time that you definitely didn't spend surfing the net? Include commuting time, time spent waiting in queues, etc. (Use different colours for different categories if you like.)

At the end of the week, calculate how much time you spent in each area. It can be a brilliant way of highlighting slots of time that could be used in other ways and for you to realize just how much you are committing to certain projects.

DECLUTTERING YOUR WEEK

Do you find yourself sitting down for your morning tea in the evening? Are you halfway up the road before you realize you've forgotten to spit out your mouthwash? Why is everything such a mad rush?

1. You're taking on too much.
2. You're not making the best use of your time.

Take a look at your time chart and ask yourself, honestly, if you're happy with the way you're spending your days. We are all guilty of trying to do too much, but if you divide your time too thinly, you won't be able to do things to the best of your ability (or look after yourself properly). Highlight at least one area of your schedule that could be improved by dropping commitments, delegating tasks or finding a more efficient way to get things done. Now do it!

PERFECT PLANNING

A good routine for your day-to-day commitments will save you valuable time.

- On Sunday, go through your diary for the week ahead. Note down anything that you need to get ready for yourself and your family members: an outfit for a party, sports kit, that hilarious inflatable banana for April Fool's Day...

- Every evening, lay out your clothes for the next day and any other items that you'll need.

- Improve your morning routine – especially if you live with others. Can you rearrange timings so that you don't end up queuing for the bathroom?

- Always put things away as you use them, put appointments in your diary immediately, and reply to emails and texts when you open them.

- If you're going up- or downstairs (or to the kitchen/ living room/wherever) don't go empty-handed. Find something that you can take with you to put away and save yourself a trip later.

MAKING TIME

It's amazing what you can do in 5 minutes... as you'll know if you've ever slept through your alarm. If you look at your day carefully, you'll soon find 5-minute slots all over the place that you can use cannily to free up more time for the fun stuff later on. While your tea is brewing, you could:

- Open and answer your post/emails/texts
- Book that dental/medical/hair appointment
- Check whose birthdays are coming up this month and order a gift online
- Go through your in-tray and file paperwork or pay a bill
- Dust/vacuum/tidy something (boring, yes – but you'll be glad when you don't have to do it later)
- Do some sit-ups
- Put on a favourite track and sing or dance along for an instant mood boost.

TIME IS THE MOST VALUABLE THING A MAN CAN SPEND.

THEOPHRASTUS

TIME IT

One sure way to help you focus on the passing of time is to use a stopwatch or kitchen timer and...

- Start it at the beginning of a "discussion". When you've had enough, check your timer and say, "We spent 13 minutes and 2 seconds discussing what kind of swimming pool the hotel should have... Shall we move on to booking the flights?"

- Force yourself to have a break: "I will sit down for 15 minutes to drink this tea while it's hot/to watch some trashy TV."

- Force yourself to do some work: "In 15 minutes, I will stop drinking this tea/watching trashy TV and do the dishes."

- End a lengthy phone call. Set a loud alarm to go off according to your boredom threshold and then say, "Sorry. Must go. Don't want my Roquefort and walnut scones to burn."

- Set yourself the challenge of completing a task in a certain amount of time, then see if you can beat it next time!

Work, Play and Sleep

We spend a lot of time at work, so it's important that our jobs are as stress-free as possible. Simplifying and organizing your working day will make your life a million times easier, and the good news is that there are plenty of ways you can improve how you work.

We all know that work has a way of leaching into our leisure hours – as overtime or worry time – so carving out an hour or two to indulge in our hobbies can be a challenge. How can you safeguard your me-time and learn to switch off at the end of a challenging day? It's actually a lot easier than you might think. Read on for some sneaky tricks to redress the work-life balance and find yourself more time to play (or sleep!).

GAIN CONTROL OF YOUR TIME, AND YOU WILL GAIN CONTROL OF YOUR LIFE.

JOHN LANDIS MASON

WORKING WELL

Whether your work is office-based, home-based or kitchen-sink-based, getting things done as efficiently as possible will leave more time for the things you enjoy. Try these tips to streamline your work time.

- Clear and organize your work area/desk if you haven't already done so.

- Identify any tasks that you dread or which drain your energy. Do you have to do these? Can they be delegated or is there an easier way to get them done? Talk to your boss or others for advice. (It's OK to ask for help!)

- Set aside a session to do the tasks that have been lurking at the bottom of your in-tray or to-do list for weeks. You'll feel so much better for clearing them in one fell swoop.

- At the end of each day, have a 5-minute tidy and declutter. Plan a longer session for the end of your week, too.

EASY INTERACTIONS

You can save a lot of time by practising clutter-free communication, whether it's via email, over the phone or in person.

- Emails: Don't check them every time a new one pops up or you'll end up flitting from task to task. Set a few longer sessions for dealing with these. Also, don't rush to check messages first thing; start your day by doing a task from your to-do list instead.

- Requests: Make these clear, polite and to the point. Always include a tactful deadline: "It would be helpful if I could have this by..." Follow up as necessary.

- Meetings: Do you really need a meeting? Is it necessary to solve a specific issue in person or is it just an excuse to sit around and eat biscuits?

- Tricky co-workers: Defuse issues before they escalate. If you experience bad behaviour, avoid confrontations, document any incidents and make a complaint to the appropriate person.

DEFENDING YOUR ME-TIME

Life is short and it's important that you factor in time to do the things you enjoy, even if you have to barricade yourself inside your (newly decluttered) shed to do it. Schedule some downtime in your diary each week. If you have wall-to-wall commitments, think about whether you really have to do everything in your diary. Will anyone notice if you take bought items along to a party rather than cooking something yourself? Can you arrange to swap child-minding or other duties with a friend if you agree to return the favour another time? If you have kids, set up a regular appointment with a childminder if possible or introduce an hour of "quiet time" at the end of each school day so that you can all unwind.

Once you've found yourself a regular slot, don't forget to plan what you want to do in that time, otherwise you'll end up drifting around, catching up on the housework or emails.

EXTRA BUBBLES EQUALS
EXTRA ENJOYMENT

A RELAXING BATH IS A
ME-TIME CLASSIC

DE-STRESSING

Learning to leave our worries behind is a skill that should be practised regularly.

1. Sit down and close your eyes. Breathe deeply. Focus on your breathing. Inhale for four counts, hold your breath for four counts and exhale for four counts – and repeat.

2. Tense and relax the muscles in your legs (starting from your feet and working your way up) and then your arms (starting with your hands). Finally, allow your neck muscles to relax.

3. Listen to the sounds around you. Concentrate on experiencing the sound, rather than thinking: "Someone's mowing their lawn... Maybe I should be mowing MY lawn..."

4. If your thoughts are drawn to a specific issue, imagine releasing it in some way (launching it like a dove, sending it out into space, etc.). Refocus on your breathing.

5. Take some time to reacclimatize gently after your meditation.

A RUFFLED MIND MAKES A RESTLESS PILLOW.

CHARLOTTE BRONTË

A GOOD NIGHT'S SLEEP

These days, thanks to our devices, we are on call 24/7. It can be harder than ever to (literally) switch off at the end of the day. Get yourself some quality zzz's by trying these tips.

- Ditch the devices – no phones, laptops or work-related paraphernalia allowed in the bedroom.
- Make your bedroom a clutter-free haven with a few luxurious touches (use aromatherapy oils or a subtle sound system).
- Treat yourself to a couple of sets of good-quality bed linen, rather than a cupboard full of cheaper items.
- Think about lighting levels (low) and room temperature (not too hot or you'll find it difficult to get up in the morning). Try to sleep with the window open (if the sounds of birds/trains/drunk passers-by won't disturb your rest).

MONEY

Everyone can benefit from streamlining their finances. By focusing on maxing your income and fine-tuning your spending, you'll end up with more pennies in the bank, as well as a warm decluttery glow. But if the thought of dusting off your calculator and checking your bank balance fills you with despair, take heart. There's no need to start Googling "places where people barter instead of using currency" – moving to a different country is actually much harder work than moving your bank account or changing your energy provider. As always, sorting your shit out will make your life easier and less stressful... and we'll do it one step at a time.

A WISE MAN
SHOULD HAVE
MONEY IN HIS
HEAD, BUT NOT
IN HIS HEART.

JONATHAN SWIFT

THE INS AND OUTS

If you've only got a hazy idea of your monthly outgoings, start by going through your bank statements for the past three months and listing your regular payments. (You could even make a spreadsheet if you're feeling super-organized or check out an online budget calculator for a pain-free way of doing this.)

It's easy enough to pick out your monthly direct debits and standing orders. Then it's a good idea to categorize the rest of your spending to get a full picture of where your money goes. (For example, did you realize that your daily decaf cappuccino was costing you that much every month?!)

The big question to ask yourself is: are you spending more than your income? If you are, now is the time to take action, and there are plenty of ways in which you can cut back and save yourself a few pounds.

DECLUTTERING YOUR SPENDING

Analyzing your monthly outgoings will highlight some obvious areas where you could be saving a penny or two.

- **Banking charges:** Make sure you have a fee-free account and check it daily to avoid going overdrawn.
- **Unused subscriptions:** Do you pay for gym membership and visit less than once a week? If so, cancel your membership and buy the odd day pass or get fit at home for free.
- **Insurance on appliances:** One policy for all your white goods can be more cost-effective than paying for separate policies. (I know, I know – this isn't as exhilarating as whitewater rafting or even clipping your fingernails, but it's still worth doing.)
- **Luxuries:** We all deserve a treat, but if you're strapped for cash, try reserving meals out for really special occasions or ditching the daily trip to the sandwich shop (you can buy your own avocados, you know).

MONEY MAINTENANCE

- **Stay up to date:** Pay everything on time and keep your records up to date. This way, you'll have the info to hand if you need to query anything or fill out any claims.

- **Consolidate your debts:** Pay off debts before syphoning any money into savings – the interest you pay on your debts will far outweigh any savings income.

- **Stagger annual payments** so that they don't all hit your account at the same time. Try to schedule them for a "good" month, when you have fewer expenses (i.e. not around Christmas!).

- **Budget** and set aside a monthly amount towards costs such as car expenses, dental bills and pet care.

- Remember that **help is at hand** if you're applying for benefits or if you need guidance in keeping your accounts. (Check online for official guidelines.)

I BEG YOU
TAKE COURAGE;
THE BRAVE
SOUL CAN MEND
EVEN DISASTER.

CATHERINE THE GREAT

It may be time-consuming (and bum-achingly boring), but an overhaul of your service providers can save you stacks of cash. With your current documents to hand, set aside a day to check out energy, TV and phone providers, and compare quotes on home and car insurance. (Then reward yourself with a little treat at the end of this gruelling session.) Incidentally, never accept an inflated automatic renewal quote. If you call your provider and threaten to move to a rival, they'll often reduce their payments to keep you sweet.

Make sure you're getting the best deal on your savings and bank accounts, too. (Open an ISA, even if you use it to save towards annual expenses.) And are you entitled to any benefits or grants? As well as the obvious ones, you may be able to claim for an energy grant or uniform rebate.

There are several useful websites that offer independent financial advice and include detailed information on how to check out all of these issues.

Study

We live such busy lives that it can be tricky to fit our studies in, stay on top of coursework and give our assignments the time they deserve. Whether you're studying for fun or for an essential qualification, being well organized will – literally – give you better results.

If you want to find out how to max your study time, get the most from your textbooks or revolutionize your revision, look no further. So stop defacing that ring binder and break open a new pack of highlighters... you're going to sort your educational shit out.

THE NOBLEST PLEASURE IS THE JOY OF UNDERSTANDING.

LEONARDO DA VINCI

THE BASICS

If you haven't already set up a dedicated study area (see page 41), do so at once! You should be able to sit down and start work straightaway, without spending 15 minutes looking for your textbooks.

Organize your notes with a ring binder for each subject. Use dividers and different coloured paper for different topics. (Use separate folders on your desktop for digital notes.)

Work out the best time of day for you to study. Are you a morning person or a night owl? Schedule study slots into your diary to suit you.

Turn off your phone and any other distracting devices before you start work – that Instagram pic of your friend's birthday party can wait until you've got to grips with the Siege of Paris (1870–71).

READING 101

Politics, performing arts, plumbing... whatever your subject, there's always going to be some reading involved – OK, a lot of reading – so you might as well do it as efficiently as possible.

1. Take a seat, adjust the lighting, turn off any electrical devices, stow your tray table and identify your emergency exits.

2. Before you start, try to remember what you already know about the topic. What do you need to find out? Jot down some notes.

3. Take a look at the title of the chapter and any sub-headings to get in the zone.

4. Read the first and last sentence of each paragraph before diving in.

5. Now read through in depth, highlighting important facts as you go. (Be selective – you don't want to end up with a sea of luminous text.)

6. Summarize the main points on a fresh sheet of paper.

IT'S ALL IN THE TIMING

Using your time wisely can have a big impact on your study success.

- Plan ahead and break your revision and assignments down into stages. Work out how long each step will take and make a start – don't put it off! You'll feel better for biting the bullet. Work in half-hour bursts, with a quick 5-minute break at the end of each.

- Think through your latest learning while doing everyday tasks, such as the dishes or walking to the shops.

- Got 10 minutes to spare? Rewrite your notes on one topic – it's a great way of remembering things. Draw a mind map; write facts out in different colours or record them and listen to them later during your commute.

- Find a patient friend with a high boredom threshold and see if you can "teach" them what you're learning. Retelling information is another good way of absorbing it.

MAKE EXAMS EASY

You've revised until your eyes bled and your brain melted. So what else can you do to make sure you pass an exam with flying colours?

1. Practise exam papers under exam conditions at home.
2. Make sure you understand the marking scheme in advance.
3. Get some sleep the night before and eat breakfast first thing.
4. Don't get wired on coffee.
5. Look over your notes before going into the exam room.
6. Go in with a positive attitude – you CAN pass.
7. Don't panic. Read all the instructions carefully... twice.
8. Once you understand the question, make sure you answer the question. (Don't regurgitate random facts.)
9. Write clearly and neatly. Check your spelling.

THE MOST
EFFECTIVE
WAY TO DO IT,
IS TO DO IT.

AMELIA EARHART

Your ideal job should challenge and inspire you. It should pay you enough money to live comfortably and offer you the chance to progress. No job is perfect, but if you're feeling stressed, trapped or undervalued in the workplace, it could be time to make a change. So what should you be doing with your life? How can you go about pursuing your dream career? And is "chocolate taster" actually a real job?

FAR AND AWAY
THE BEST PRIZE
THAT LIFE HAS
TO OFFER IS THE
CHANCE TO WORK
HARD AT WORK
WORTH DOING.

THEODORE ROOSEVELT

SHOULD I STAY OR SHOULD I GO?

Do you know someone who is unhappy in their job? Someone who is endlessly banging on about their poor pay or tedious duties? Is that person you? At its worst, workplace stress can damage your relationships, emotional well-being and health. If you wake up dreading your working day, you have three options (and notice that "putting up with things" is not one of them!).

1. **Same place, different role:** Can your current job be adapted or could you transfer to a different department? Don't suffer in silence; talk to your boss.

2. **Different place, same role:** If you like what you're doing but not where you're doing it, check out other options in the industry. Use your contacts to help you.

3. **Different place, different role:** If you feel queasy every time you clock in, put on your thinking cap – or mortar board or safety helmet – because it's time for a change... The world is your bivalve mollusc.

CHOICES, CHOICES

Barrister or barista? How do you choose the right career for you? You should be familiar with the sort-your-shit-out approach by now – reach for a piece of paper (or suitable electronic device) and start with a brainstorm. Think about the following questions.

- What do you like and dislike about your current role?
- Which working environment suits you best?
- Do you prefer to work alone or as part of a team?
- What are your strengths?
- Which work-related activities do you love doing?
- What did you want to be when you were a child?
- Which of your friends' careers do you envy and why?

If you're still drawing a blank, try an online careers questionnaire or visit a careers adviser. (Some websites offer free consultations with an online adviser.)

MOVING ON

You've decided you definitely want a career in agriculture, what with the fresh air and all that, so what's next? Set aside some time each day to work on Project New Beginning, and...

1. **Research your chosen job:** Find out everything you can. (It's not all about wandering through meadows, you know.) Surf the net, talk to people who work in the industry and read the trade press.

2. **Get some experience:** Work shadow, volunteer, take an evening class or stalk a farmer.

3. **Be enthusiastic!** If you've researched the pants off your dream job and love what you see, pour that enthusiasm into your applications and let it shine during interviews. You'll win your new employer over no problem at all.

4. **Good luck!**

DECLUTTERING YOUR RÉSUMÉ

A clear, accurate and well-presented résumé will catch any employer's eye. Make sure that it wings its way to the top of the pile by following these simple rules.

- **Make it concise:** Don't go over the top with lengthy personal statements or reams of information about courses and summer jobs. Pick out the relevant points and present these in a way that will make them stand out at a glance.

- **Make it clear:** Avoid novelty fonts or anything that's tricky to read. Pick something that's easy on the eye (and don't print your résumé on coloured paper). Include clearly defined sections, but don't go to town with too many different styles of heading, etc.

- **Make it mistake-free:** Check it, check it and check it again; then ask a friend to proofread it too (especially if spelling and grammar aren't your strong points).

ACING AN INTERVIEW

Everyone has a "worst interview" story, and they do have great comedy value, but avoid adding a new tale to your repertoire by following these tips.

1. Prepare: **Research the company and check out their product (if relevant).**

2. Arrive on time and be polite to everyone: **Scowl at the receptionist and you may well have failed before you've begun.**

3. Greet your interviewer(s) **with a confident, friendly smile and a firm handshake.**

4. Keep your body language under control: **Sit up straight and tall in your chair, relax your shoulders and hands, and you'll look – and feel – calmer and more confident.**

5. Answer questions fully but without waffling: **A silence does not need to be filled by you with an anecdote about your last boss.**

6. Show genuine interest in the business: **Ask a specific (and relevant!) question about how something works within the company.**

Health and Fitness

When it comes to sorting your shit out, health and fitness is an area that many of us want to tackle, and the good news is that you really don't need to find hours and hours every week to do it. Small changes – when included in your daily routine – can have big results. If you've already decluttered your surroundings, you'll already be feeling lighter and brighter, so imagine how fantastic you'll feel when you've decluttered your diet and organized your fitness regime too.

There are lots of speedy tips and tricks that you can use to tweak your diet and boost your fitness levels – and the more you do, the better you'll feel. Even if you haven't yet given your diet or fitness a moment's notice, don't despair. You don't have a mountain to climb – you just have even more fun new things to try.

IF WE COULD GIVE
EVERY INDIVIDUAL
THE RIGHT AMOUNT
OF NOURISHMENT
AND EXERCISE, NOT
TOO LITTLE AND
NOT TOO MUCH,
WE WOULD HAVE
FOUND THE SAFEST
WAY TO HEALTH.

HIPPOCRATES

GET MOTIVATED

Take a few moments to picture the healthiest version of yourself that you can. What's different about you? Perhaps you have a more toned physique. Your skin is glowing (in a good way) and your hair is thick and glossy. Maybe you've got more energy and you're bounding up the stairs like a gazelle in a high-rise? You're looking fantastic, and as a result, you're bursting with confidence, energy and enthusiasm. And maybe, just maybe, you're feeling a teensy bit happier?!

So how do you achieve this picture of health and loveliness? We all know that two of the most important things to get to this stage are eating well and exercising more. But how do you fit that into your busy schedule? Easily! Just:

1. Take small steps to reach your goals
2. Make them a part of your routine and they'll become second nature.

DIET DECLUTTER

Changing your diet won't just have a positive impact on how you look; it will also change how you feel, as a poor diet can leave you feeling tired and drained. With too much processed food to eliminate and not enough good stuff to run on, our bodies will struggle to get us through the day.

The most important thing you can do is to drink more water. You know the facts: our bodies are made up of 70 per cent water, all our bodily functions need it to work properly and if you feel thirsty, you are already dehydrated. Drinking water – around 2 litres (eight glasses) a day – will boost your immune system, brain power, energy levels, looks and mood. It will also prevent illness and headaches. And, yes, you'll have to pee more, but hey, that's some extra exercise and a change of scenery, so it's win-win.

FOOD SWAPS

Plan ahead and shop carefully to make sure you have more nutritious food options to hand.

Ditch the...	Restock with...
Ready meals (a longer ingredients list means lower nutritional value)	Speedy stir-fry ingredients and steamed fish and veg – or prepare stews and casseroles ahead in a slow cooker.
Crisps, nuts and biscuits (high in saturated fats and salt)	Raisins, unsweetened dried fruit, etc. Chop crudités and serve with hummus.
Caffeinated drinks (too much can cause heart problems, insomnia and stress)	Decaf alternatives, herbal teas and... hello, are you drinking more water yet?!
Cakes, sweets, confectionery (loaded with refined sugar)	Plain yoghurt and a touch of honey, a square or two of dark chocolate and soft fruit, such as plums and nectarines.

HEALTH FIXES

Feel better instantly with these quick fixes.

- **Breathe properly:** Most of us snatch shallow breaths and do not take in enough oxygen to benefit our body. Practise breathing deep into your lungs and you'll immediately feel energized.
- **Take a quick break and...**
  - walk round the block
  - have a power nap (no more than 20 minutes)
  - do a whole-body relaxation exercise (see page 110).
- **Laugh:** Watch a clip of your favourite comedy or text a friend who always makes you smile. Laughter boosts your mood. (There are even local laughter groups in some areas where you can meet up and laugh yourselves silly!)

HE WHO LAUGHS, LASTS!

MARY PETTIBONE POOLE

GET MOVING

If your heart sinks at the thought of joining a gym, don't worry! Here are some alternatives.

- **Walking or cycling instead of driving:** Walk wherever you can – you'll be surprised at your daily distances. Get a pedometer (or an app on your phone) and watch the kilometres clock up.
- **Taking the stairs instead of the lift:** It's obvious, but it gets results. Do it regularly and you'll soon be jogging – not panting – your way up.
- Martial arts, trampolining, pole-dancing: Try one of the multitude of fitness classes available. Don't be shy – your instructor and new comrades will make you feel welcome. You *are* feeling shy? Well, why not try out some moves at home first with an online tutorial.

HONE IT AT HOME

Even half an hour spent working out at home can produce great results. Try these quick fitness fixes while watching your favourite soap. (Don't forget to warm up with some stretches first.)

- **Hula hooping:** Great for toning. Anyone can do it with the right-sized hoop. (It must be as wide as the distance from your hip to the floor.)
- **Body blitz:** Pick an area of your body to tone and find a 2-minute workout online. Make it part of your daily routine.
- **Kettlebell:** A cheap (and small) piece of equipment for all-over body toning. There are lots of different exercises you can try. Use a lighter weight (3–6 kg) and more reps for toning or a heavier weight (8–12 kg) and fewer reps for building muscle.

You should see results in four weeks and soon your friends will comment on how great you're looking!

LET IT GO

Decluttering our emotions is as important as looking after ourselves physically. Negative feelings are natural reactions to everyday situations, but if you don't release them, you'll end up getting so stressed that you'll blow up in the supermarket when someone jumps the queue.

- **Venting:** Phone a sympathetic friend and have a good rant. (Make sure that they are up for your rant-a-thon first, though.) If your friend is also stressed, encourage them to rant too. It's the rant rather than the response that helps.

- **Physical activity:** Dance around the room, sing along to a favourite track or go for a run.

- **Experience the great outdoors:** Get some fresh air and a fresh perspective. (That squirrel doesn't look stressed, does he?)

- **Tapping:** Tapping acupressure points releases stress. There are many practitioners around, but an effective DIY option is tapping the area just beneath the collarbone.

LOVE AND FRIENDSHIP

Friends are there for the good times, the bad times and the times when we can't remember how we got home, so they have to give us a carefully edited recap of our missing hours. Nothing has more of an impact on us than the way we relate to those around us. Our relationships bring joy to our lives, so how can we make the most of them? And nothing hurts more than a relationship in trouble, so how can we fix things when they go wrong?

MY FRIENDS ARE MY ESTATE.

EMILY DICKINSON

KEEP YOUR FRIENDSHIPS ACTIVE

Make sure that you share quality time with your friends by regularly planning something specific – and fun – to do together. Why not try one of the following ideas?

- **Learn something new:** Whether it's rock climbing or pottery, a sailing trip or a karaoke session, the experience will bring you closer together.

- **Make an open invitation:** Phone your friend and ask them what they have always wanted to do. You might end up trying something you've never considered before.

- **Throw a party together:** You could be celebrating your friendship, a birthday – or nothing in particular. (Who needs a reason for a party?!)

- **Plan a wild night in:** Invite your friend over for dinner and spend the night eating, drinking, playing board games or watching your favourite movies.

THE GOLDEN RULES

Keep all your relationships happy and healthy by following these five golden rules.

1. **Be yourself:** Pretence in any relationship is a recipe for disaster.

2. **Don't expect other people to change:** It won't happen (or if it does, it won't last!).

3. **Treat your friends as you would want to be treated yourself:** Listen to the way you speak to others and what you say.

4. **Make sure your friendships are a two-way street:** Are you the only one making the effort? Balanced relationships should involve give and take.

5. **Be present:** The greatest gift you can give a friend when you are together is your attention. Active listening is a great skill to practise, so try to focus on real-world communication and turn off your phone when you're spending quality time with your friends.

EXCESS BAGGAGE

No relationship is perfect, but if you often feel drained after catching up with one of your pals, your friendship may need some attention. It's natural to want to support our friends, but make sure that you don't end up in a supporting role all the time. If you are constantly feeling stressed after hearing the latest details of your friend's break-up/house move/night out fiasco, it's a warning sign that your friendship is out of kilter.

Limit the time you spend in this role: you are not doing your friend any favours in the long run if they become dependent on you as an outlet for their woes. Listen and offer advice if asked, but don't take their worries away with you. Your friend may lay their troubles at your door, but you don't need to pick them up and add them to your own burden. (It's also important to make sure that you're not overburdening your friends in the same way. Don't become someone else's excess baggage!)

BUILDING BRIDGES

We all have the odd niggle in our friendships, but what can you do if things escalate? How can you patch up an argument?

1. Be honest with yourself about why you've fallen out.

2. Try to see your friend's point of view, too. Taking time to do this can transform the way you respond to the situation.

3. Write down how you feel (on a piece of paper, not a device with a "send" button). Offloading will make you feel better and help you to reevaluate what's happened.

4. Talk to an impartial friend and get some perspective.

5. If you're ready to offer an olive branch, text your pal and suggest meeting up for a chat. Make it clear that you want to move forward.

6. Meet on neutral territory, stay calm and describe your feelings (without reenacting them!). Ask how your friend is feeling, too.

7. Be prepared to agree to disagree, if need be.

LOOKING FOR LOVE

Sorting our shit out usually involves decluttering and careful planning to achieve our goals, but when it comes to looking for love, it's time for a different approach. Declutter by all means – no one should be dragging enough baggage from a previous relationship to fill a seven-piece luggage set – but once you're over your ex, your mission is not to go forth into the streets and leap on the first available passer-by. In fact, you shouldn't be leaping on anyone at all. A decluttered heart may feel empty at first, but you don't need to find a rest-of-your-life soulmate to fill it with happiness.

Your mission is to go out and live life to the full. Do the things you love. Make new friends who love doing those things too and you'll be so busy enjoying yourself that you won't have time to think about whether Mr or Mrs Right will appear. Finding a partner may not be your end goal after all, but whatever your goal is, you should be having too much fun to worry about a deadline.

COUPLE MAINTENANCE

Like bicycles and boilers, relationships require regular maintenance. You can't run them into the ground for decades and expect to avoid the odd puncture or leaky valve. Keep things fresh with these tips.

- **Dating:** You've lived together for years, so you don't need to go out to meet up, but spending quality time together is super-important. (And no talking about retiling the roof!)

- **Be surprising:** Write your partner a love note or cook them a meal... Just don't be too surprising! "I've sold the flat – we're going to live in a lighthouse," may be a step too far.

- **Visit new places:** Going somewhere new together will freshen up your dynamic, as you'll both be on unfamiliar territory.

- **Set a new goal:** Couples often stop having goals once they've ticked the obvious ones off the list. Strengthen your partnership with a new dream to pursue together.

Conclusion

You should only need to declutter your home once... as long as you don't reclutter it, of course. Once you've waved goodbye to all your excess belongings and experienced the benefits of living a streamlined lifestyle, you'll have a great incentive to keep things running smoothly. Just remember:

1. Always put things away after using them.
2. If things don't have a place, find them one or get rid!

Take care not to acquire too much new stuff to replace your old clutter. When you're thinking about buying something new, ask yourself these simple questions:

1. Will I use it or will it enhance my life? Are you buying a laser tape measure because you need to take lots of measurements? Or are you buying it because you'd quite like to be the sort of person who owns a laser tape measure?

2. **Where will I put it?** Can you picture a space for your potential purchase at home? If not, don't buy it. Go home and prepare a space first!

Follow these rules and it will be easy to keep your home clutter-free, but don't forget to do the same with your personal life. Now that you've freed up some time for your hobbies, make sure that you don't spend it taking on extra chores or responsibilities instead.

Remember that routine is your friend. If you want to make a change to your life, make it a part of your routine in any way you can. (A lifestyle change – such as starting a new job or the kids changing schools – can be a good time to introduce other changes to your routine, too.)

Regularly reassess your plans and priorities; don't wait for New Year to think about your goals. When you sit down (hopefully with your feet up) at the start of the week to plan ahead, take a moment to look back at the previous week, too. Did you meet the careers adviser for advice about retraining? Did you set aside time to try that new dance class? If the answer is no, remind yourself why you set these goals. Find an even more prominent place to pin up your list of goals and take a step towards the first one tomorrow.

Most of all, remember that if you sort your shit out, you can change any aspect of your life for the better. You can move mountains if you want to – especially now that you have the time to do it. All you have to do is pick up your spade.

TELL ME,
WHAT IS IT
YOU PLAN TO
DO WITH YOUR
ONE WILD AND
PRECIOUS LIFE?

MARY OLIVER

Less is More

FINDING JOY IN
A SIMPLER LIFE

Robin James
Hardback
978-1-78783-577-1

Discover the art of finding more through having less: more time, more calm, more energy, more money, more *you*.

Filled with practical tips and ideas, this book will guide you toward a simpler way of life. Learn how to reduce your clutter and your stress levels, find advice on mastering your schedule and making time for what matters, and enrich your everyday by putting quality before quantity.

From time to time, we all get lost in the flurry of a busy life, but we can always uncover a path back to our best and happiest selves. All you need is focus, a slower pace and the simple power of "less".

How to Tidy Your Mind

REDUCE MENTAL CLUTTER AND FIND CALM

Anna Barnes
Paperback
978-1-80007-408-8

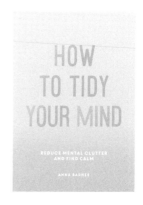

A tidy mind is a calm mind. Through a series of easy-to-follow tips, this book will help you clear your mental clutter, improve your clarity and find peace.

Do you ever feel frazzled and unable to concentrate? Are you drained by the never-ending to-do list in your head? Would you like to feel more in control? If the answer is "yes", you are not alone – and it might be time to give your mind a spring clean.

Mental clutter is anything in your head that takes up time and energy, and when there's too much, the mind becomes exhausted. But with a few simple techniques, you can bring order to your inner world and find a sense of peace again.

Have you enjoyed this book? If so, find us on Facebook at Summersdale Publishers, on Twitter/X at @Summersdale and on Instagram and TikTok at @summersdalebooks and get in touch. We'd love to hear from you!

www.summersdale.com

IMAGE CREDITS

Cover and pp.3, 8, 87 © Martial Red/Shutterstock.com; p.10 © Nadiinko/Shutterstock.com; pp.13, 20, 23, 47, 55, 58, 63, 68, 73, 109, 153, illustrations by Konstiantyn Fedorov; p.29 © Ahm 1275/Shutterstock.com; p.31 © owatta/Shutterstock.com; p.42 © Kolesnikov Vladimir/Shutterstock.com; p.50 © AnyaLis/Shutterstock.com; p.63 © espresso1993/Shutterstock.com; p.71 © Kibets Olena/Shutterstock.com; p.76 ball © AbdulMalix/Shutterstock.com, bear © MariMuz/Shutterstock.com; p.80 © Artrise Stocker/Shutterstock.com; p.92 © everything bagel/Shutterstock.com; p.104 © Panda Vector/Shutterstock.com; p.113 © Polina Tomtosova/Shutterstock.com; p.120 © Progdiz/Shutterstock.com; p.127 © My Flat Style/Shutterstock.com; p.144 © nubenamo/Shutterstock.com; p.147 © Semanche/Shutterstock.com; p.156 © ids design/Shutterstock.com